"*I have gone through all the exciting sensations of creating a garden, beginning with a packet of sweet alyssum and a packet of radishes bought at a local hardware store when I was seven.*"

"*One of the first gardens I did outside the family was for the designer Hattie Carnegie. I was 23 then, and I went to her salon, but could not afford any of her dresses myself, though I loved them. Miss Carnegie suggested I do a garden in exchange for a coat and dress, and so I designed and planted a garden for her.*"

—RACHEL LAMBERT MELLON, AKA BUNNY MELLON

"Every garden has its own way of being. Its own atmosphere."

"The sky is a free asset in design
            and nothing unnecessary should be
       planted that takes away the sky."

"The quality of a garden does not depend on size. Gardens are personal reflections of the taste, hopes, and desires of each maker. They can be a small backyard, or they can go as far as the eye can see."

"Everyone starts in a different way.
    I am not going to discuss rooftop gardening,
as I have had little experience."

"The creation of a garden is the work and thoughts of many minds. Like a piece of cloth, it is woven of numerous threads."

"A garden isn't always an outlined area.
A garden is all the space—
the landscape that is yours to put together."

"Gardening is a way of life. As long as I can remember,
I have never been without a plant or something growing."

"Start in a small way" and watch.

Beginning

Butter Cups –

"Allow plants to roam a bit, like clouds that float over an organized design lasting three weeks or so. Then cut back and watch where they seed for another year."

"Seeds are a wonderment."

Lavender → Favorite Flower
Red & Purple. This Summer. Called
"Bee Balm."

"Ideas and imagination make every garden different. Like any work of art, each individual has his own way of doing."

"I have been a gardener ever since I can remember.
When I was six years old, to my mother's dismay,
I started stealing plants. It has been an unceasing interest
that leads one into the world of books, of history,
of nature, and of fascinating people."

"It must be in harmony with the elements that are going to contain it."

"I am not an educated botanist, horticulturist, or landscape gardener. However, without formal training I have earned and enjoyed in a self-taught fashion all its pleasures and satisfactions. That is why for all of you who want to open this door, it is there for the taking."

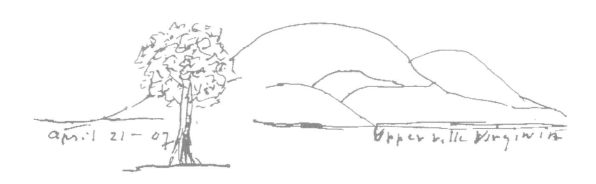

"I always design a landscape with fixed horizons, whether it be mountains or a stone wall around a 20-foot-square plot."

"Part of creating is understanding that there is always more to do; nothing is ever completely finished."

Virginia
Mts — 
5. March

A dove in a far away
forest tree calling
in the snow —

Love
Your Friend

"All I really care is something turns out well. Then I can turn to the next."

"I feel public gardens as well as private should have
 an atmosphere that inspires and one can relate to.
There must always be a feeling people can take home,
even copy, or remember later with a positive
 and thoughtful recall."

"A gardener plans at least eighteen months ahead."

Orange Tree with New shoots

"Too much should not be explained about a garden.
Its greatest reality is not reality,
for a garden, hovering always in a state of becoming,
sums its own past and its future."

My Bird on Top of
the Chinianji.

"To keep a garden is to create,
to dream, and to hope."

"A garden, like a library, is a whole made up of separate interests and mysteries.
Among these mysteries are green flowers and the shaping of some herbs into small trees."

"It is usually more than one person who creates a garden. It is the weaving together of ideas."

Dearest Robert —

Your coming down has made all the difference —

Blue eyed grass +
daisies. Wild
flowers

old Orange Tree.

"This library, which includes manuscripts going back to the 1300s, amounts to a working collection, for it is in continuous use.
    From it I learned much about pruning, growing, and designing, for past methods were often ahead of ours."

"Flowers are the paint box of the garden."

"There is a different rhythm for every design."

"As I see things, the past is my reference book—
 like a pear tree along the road with wild violets passed
by quickly can find its echo years later in a simple landscape."

"As a child, wildflowers were part of
my feeling of freedom."

Swamp Flowers –

"The intense, bright color of buttercups
made me think that if I had to live
alone in a cellar room, I would paint it
yellow and never miss the sun."

upperville - Virginia

"Trees make patterns
on the ground like lace."

By Th Sea
Cold + Blue.

"Countless imaginative creations have found their expression in flowers, and the cycle of their life has the strength of sensual pleasure with their scent, fruits, and seeds."

23 22 21 20   6 5 4 3 2

Copyright © 2020 Linda Jane Holden, Bryan Huffman, and Thomas Lloyd

Front cover: *Fritillaria pallidiflora*
Back cover: *Laurel, Butcher's Broom (Ruscus hypoglossum)*
The front and back cover images are 17th-century French school oil paintings, artist unknown, from a pharmacy in the Loire Valley. It is interesting to note that the roots are depicted in the paintings because of the medicinal applications of the plants. Bunny Mellon acquired the oil paintings, which hung in her Oak Spring Garden Library. Photographs courtesy Oak Spring Garden Library.

Illustrations throughout are by Bunny Mellon,
from personal letters and notes sent to family and friends.
Illustrations © Thomas Lloyd, Gerard B. Lambert Foundation

All rights reserved. No part of this book may be reproduced by any means whatsoever without written permission from the publisher, except brief portions quoted for purpose of review.

Published by
Gibbs Smith
P.O. Box 667
Layton, Utah 84041

1.800.835.4993 orders
www.gibbs-smith.com

Designed by Rita Sowins / Sowins Design
Printed and bound in China

Gibbs Smith books are printed on either recycled, 100% post-consumer waste, FSC-certified papers or on paper produced from sustainable PEFC-certified forest/controlled wood source. Learn more at www.pefc.org.

ISBN: 978142365539-8